Toxic Relationships

How to Identify an Unhealthy Relationship and Take Action to Repair It or Free Yourself

by Devin Walters

Table of Contents

Introduction

One of the most important aspects of our lives is the people we relate with. As social creatures, we simply have the need to interact with one another for various reasons. We need these people to be the kind that we can trust, talk to, and find comfort in. These people also become part of our lives to various degrees, as friends, family, co-workers and, most importantly, our "significant other."

Whatever it is that you may call your relationship with another person, it goes without saying that it must be one that works. That is, it has to be the kind that makes you both happy and helps you grow as individuals. As you've probably experienced yourself, not all the people you've had relationships with were good for you. Some of your friends can be mildly irritating, while others are just so unbearable that they already begin to weigh down on your self-esteem. When not dealt with properly and immediately, they will begin to affect your daily life and even impact on how you relate with other people in your life.

Sure, no relationship is ever perfect. Sometimes you even need to strike a compromise in order to build a potentially good relationship into what it could be. But when someone—you thought was important to you—starts to do more harm than good to you and the people around you, it's time to make a change before it's too late.

If you happen to be the kind of person who can tell whether a relationship you are in is healthy or not, then consider yourself lucky. Statistically, the people who are in the worst relationships are not even aware of it. Even the most obvious abusive relationships are often not apparent to the victim. That's why this guide's first objective is to help these people, maybe even you, become more aware of the real condition of their relationships. Without this kind of awareness, nothing can be done.

While there's never a guarantee, even the seemingly hopeless relationships can be saved. That's why this guide will also aim to show you what steps you can take in order to patch up problems before things escalate beyond repair. This will be one of the most challenging aspects of a relationship but if it indeed, can be saved, then this guide can make it all worthwhile.

Keep in mind though that not all relationships should be saved. Sometimes, you just need to be able to sever ties with someone because it's hurting you too much, one way or another. And as we all know, letting go of the people we are closest to can be very difficult. In fact, it can sometimes be dangerous when not done properly. Hopefully you'll never have to go through a dangerous separation, but if you do, it's important that this guide shows you how to get out without physical harm, and with as minimal emotional damage as possible. Otherwise, the separation could have serious repercussions and leave you worse off than before.

Finally, this guide will help you come to terms with the fact that not all of your relationships are good for you. While most of the discussion here will apply to romantic couples, you can certainly apply this to the closest of your family and friends. Not only will you learn about the kind of relationships you have, but it may also show you that you deserve better.

Chapter 1: Recognizing the Signs

The first step to dealing with toxic relationships is knowing how to spot them. But many people are not aware of what a healthy relationship is and what isn't. There are two extremes. On the one hand, not seeing the signs of a healthy relationship doesn't mean that it's a toxic one. On the other hand, not seeing signs of a toxic relationship doesn't mean that everything is going fine. That's why there are two separate lists to evaluate them: one that you should view as ideal to move towards, and another to avoid.

In a nutshell, most people will describe, healthy or unhealthy relationships as those that make you happy or sad, respectively. But the words "happy" and "sad" are so broad that they're not reliable benchmarks for objectively assessing a relationship. After all, sometimes we don't even know if we're happy or not. That's why these concrete signs are so important.

Signs of a Healthy Relationship

1. **You can talk to each other about anything.** Remember that feeling when you hesitated about whether you should tell someone about something? You don't get that feeling in a

healthy relationship. You're just so comfortable with this person that you can tell him/her anything. It's not that you think you'll get a positive reaction every time, but you trust that both of you are willing to deal with whatever it is.

This doesn't necessarily mean you'll be talking all the time. It simply means that your partner or friend will always be there, ready to lend an ear, no matter how weird, shocking, awkward, or even boring your ideas may be.

2. **You both have space.** "Independent and in love," some would say. Just because the two of you are in a close, committed relationship this doesn't mean that you have to spend every single moment together. And this just doesn't mean being able to have some alone time, which we all admittedly need. More importantly, this means being able to work, study, and pursue your ambitions without being dragged down by someone else. It's not that you would mind factoring in someone else in your decision making, but it's that you don't feel pressured to do so.

3. **You argue.** At face value, it doesn't seem as though arguing is supposed to be a sign of a good, working relationship. Fighting certainly isn't. But having disagreements is an indicator that you're both considering each other's dispositions. Many couples find it quite natural to air their personal views, and don't expect the partner to always agree. Of course, it's equally important that when you both disagree, you do so on fair and equal terms. That means no name-calling, making unnecessary remarks, or playing dirty. Most importantly, you notice that you argue, not because you want to prove yourself right, but because you want to understand where the other person is coming from—and that's where relationships grow.

4. **You help each other grow as people.** You give each other good advice. You listen to each other's warnings. You make it your personal goal to become a better person not only because you want your significant other to have a better you, but because you know your partner will do the same as well. And in the end, both of you win. The growth from a disagreement is especially apparent in those little things that you do for each other. Neither of you settle for mediocrity—you want to give nothing but the best to each

other. And more often than not, that's something really special.

5. **You share your feelings freely.** More than just talking, you have an understanding that you are sure of how important this person really is to you. You're not afraid to say (or imply through your gestures and expression) things like "I love you", "thank you", or "I'm sorry", may it be in public or in private. This promotes a healthy relationship because you are both certain as to where you stand and where you're headed. This is a kind of maturity you will not always see in other couples or people in general.

Signs of a Toxic Relationship

1. **There's a lot of hostility.** It doesn't have to be direct confrontation. Relationships that are going bad will often make you feel like there's some cause for you to fight just around the corner. Ever felt that your partner was already angry at you barely five minutes after you got home? Sure, a healthy relationship has its disagreements, but in these instances, you don't even know what you're fighting about anymore.

Some people go passive-aggressive, which is equally bad. This could even be you. It happens when something your partner said or did makes you upset but for some reason you don't feel as though it's okay to say so directly. So you end up just venting your frustration indirectly, causing ever more vague hostility.

2. **You feel like the relationship focuses only on one of you.** This is one of those times when the dominant-submissive relationship is taken way too far. Your partner will either make everything about him/her, or he/she will make everything about you. So you're either having to adjust to your partner's demands all the time or your partner is clinging on to you like the world depends on it.

Sometimes this behavior seems positive, such as when your partner pushes you to excel at your job and gives you all the unconditional love and support you need—until you realize it's too much. Then it becomes toxic. The bottom line? Whatever the situation is, you can't seem to breathe anymore.

3. **Change seems to be a bad thing.** Things go really bad when you don't get to go on your usual Saturday night dinners for some legitimate reason. Or maybe you can't seem to convince your partner to move to another apartment. There's a lot of fear and insecurity and both of you can't seem to leave your comfort zones anymore to do anything different, meet new people, or even consider changing lifestyles. Well the thing about relationships that you should keep in mind is that they should change—for the better. You're in a relationship where change isn't welcome at all.

4. **You can't seem to find room to grow.** Relationships are meant to help you become better as you would help your partner get better. In toxic relationships, not only does your partner bring you down a lot. You must understand that without any kind of moral support there is no relationship at all.

5. **You seem to hesitate to show your partner to other people in your life.** Maybe you've talked about wanting to meet each other's parents or hanging out with each other's friends but your partner either disagrees or something in you tells you that it's a bad idea.

This goes two ways. One, your partner could have no intentions of being part of your real life because he or she doesn't want to be accountable to the other people that matter to you. Or two, there's something about the person you're with that you know will be unacceptable to the other people in your life, although you can't put your finger on it. Maybe it's time to assess if there's really some value in being with this person.

Both lists can actually be much longer, but the items listed above should at least give you a pretty good idea as to what makes a healthy or toxic relationship tick—whether as a beating heart or as a time bomb. As you go through fixing what could be or is already a toxic relationship, you need to keep the ideals and the worst case scenarios in mind, so you can actively avoid the latter as the signs become more apparent.

Chapter 2: Different Kinds of Toxic Relationships

While they have their common signs, toxic relationships come in all shapes and sizes. This is the main reason why they are difficult to spot. Sometimes the rest of the relationship could seem fine but there's this one aspect that just screams toxicity, and you end up tolerating it because you think it's just a small part of the bigger picture. Sadly, toxic relationships eventually become the picture, and the longer you let the toxic instances go on, the harder it gets to deal with.

And knowing what it is exactly that you're dealing with is half the battle. While there might be too many variations of a toxic relationship to mention, the list below should help you become familiar with the most common ones.

The Perfectionists. Indeed, there's something good about dating a perfectionist, but there are those who let their personality get out of hand. You'll notice that they will start insisting on a way of doing things every time. It will start with something small like dates but eventually your partner is going to start meddling even with your own affairs. He/she will have a way of doing every single thing until you're surprised that a rulebook about your relationship hasn't been published yet. But it gets really bad when your partner starts taking note of your own imperfections, eventually making you feel like you're never good enough. If so, then why are you still hanging out with each other, anyway?

The Jealous Partners. A bit of jealousy can be cute sometimes, but it can get really ugly very fast, e.g. when a big fuse blows because you so much as just look at another human being; or you can't go places without your partner demanding a full report on where you've been, who you've been with, and what you did. In toxic relationships he/she still gets mad even though you didn't really do anything wrong. Sure it's important to open up to your partner about your whereabouts, but this is something that's supposed to come naturally and voluntarily. Otherwise, personal space, which is very important in relationships, becomes violated. A healthy relationship involves people trusting each other, and jealousy is the opposite of that.

The Abusive Partner. Absolutely gone are the days when society thought it was perfectly okay for a decent human being to hit another. Today, we call that violence. It's pretty much clear as crystal when it comes to physical violence: don't ever be with anyone who thinks they can just slap you or hurt you physically in any way. But abuse can come in non-physical forms as well, and that's much harder to distinguish. Verbal abuse is just as common as its physical counterpart, although they sometimes look like the typical argument couples have. It can also come in the form of economic or social exploitation. But whatever shape or form, a person who abuses you is one who thinks of you as someone who is not his or her equal, and that's not a healthy relationship.

The Liars and Cheaters. These people are just as bad as the abusers. While they don't exploit you directly, they take for granted whatever trust and confidence you have in them. While it's okay to have secrets in a relationship, people who not only keep too much from their partners but also fabricate truths about themselves will only disappoint you in the end. People who cheat on you are the ones who lie to you the most, because they basically lie about the fact that they really care about you. Remember that all sorts of people lie and cheat—friends, relatives, lovers, and even business partners. If you can't even trust them, why are you with them?

The Excessive Competitor. Partners are supposed to bring out the best in each other by inspiring each other to be better persons. But when your partner's idea of becoming better is to show how he or she is superior to you in life, the inspiration is just wrong. A loving relationship recognizes the strengths and weaknesses of each other. The reason why we need each other is because we know that we just can't do everything on our own. When someone refuses to recognize your strengths and plays up his or her own too much, that person reeks of insecurity and possibly some kind of abuse. If you're not careful, you might end up believing your partner and you'll never be able to find fault in him/her—even when there are blatant faults.

The Extreme Pessimist. At the other end of the competitor's emotional spectrum are the guys or girls who think so little of themselves that they can't even function anymore. You probably met this person at a time when you thought all that vulnerability and unassuming personality was just adorable. You thought you could help him/her overcome this, and that's how you became close to each other. Indeed, some relationships blossom that way. But pretty soon all that self-loathing becomes so unhealthy that the person seems to collapse without your guidance. Nothing you say seems to make the person feel better—he/she doesn't believe in your encouragement anymore or, worse, breaks down at the slightest criticism. People like that will be all over you, needing you like there's no tomorrow. And if you don't get some breathing space soon, there might not be a tomorrow for you.

The Manipulators. This is a tricky one. In relationships, we often let our friends and partners influence our choices. After all, compromise is a very important thing in relationships. But these people cross the line when they abuse their capacity for persuasion for their selfish benefit, especially when it's at the expense of the relationship. You're lucky if you can see the manipulation, such as when your partner uses emotional blackmail. The worst kinds are those when you don't realize that you're being manipulated, such as when he or she tries to turn you against your friends or family members. A healthy relationships is a place where you can be safe when you're vulnerable, and manipulators take advantage of that scenario. Some of these people will even claim to have your best interests at heart. But even if they do mean well, they shouldn't be achieving those ends behind your back if you're ever to be in a healthy, trusting relationship.

Remember that the list mentioned here is not exhaustive because there are as many types of toxic relationships as there are people getting together as friends, family, or lovers. The ones mentioned above, however, are not only common but are known to be dangerous as well. If you start seeing the signs, it's time to take action.

Chapter 3: Saving the Relationship

Of all the people you could possibly choose to be close to in your life, there has to be a good reason why you're with one person over another, right? And whatever those reasons are—and you shouldn't ever be judged for that—they will, most likely, be the same reasons why you will want to preserve the relationship as much as possible. This is a very important mindset in this world where we know that no relationship is ever perfect, and despite all the imperfections your friend, relative, or spouse may have, the last thing you should ever consider is cutting ties with that person. After all, you saw something good in the person initially, right?

There are many situations where relationships are toxic but can still be repaired. For instance, the toxicity may be inadvertent. You or your partner may not be aware of some habits or situations that may be causing the problem. It could also be that both of you are undergoing something drastic in your lives. In these situations, the toxicity can still be cured because the parties involved are not inherently toxic. Chances are, they would want to change to be better if they could. As the person reading this guide, it will be your goal to let that change happen.

And because you both still want to maintain the relationship, the first thing that you need to achieve is co-operation. You both have to go through this together. Through open and appropriate means of communication, you can do a number of things:

- Admit that there is a problem and see if there's anything that can be done about it. Here, it's important that both of you be objective about what really goes on when things get toxic. How does it start? What is it always about?

- Discuss certain developments about the relationship as well as your individual lives, making it possible to see if the problem is caused by something external (i.e. problem with work, family, etc.).

- Identify triggers that you can both avoid. Sometimes there are just some things you ought not to say about the other person, and you both need to respect those as any other boundary in your relationship. There are also times when the problems are due to bad timing. When was the last time you asked yourself if it's the right time to bring something up?

- Discuss what both of you ought to do when things get out of hand. The awareness alone can stop many arguments from escalating to something that could ruin the relationship. Setting ground rules will help make arguments healthier and more constructive.

Ultimately, this phase is all about coming together on clear and equal terms, with both of you understanding that you could have caused the problem together. This is also the perfect time for you assess yourself because you could be contributing to the problem as well. The good thing about admitting your own vulnerabilities to your partner at a time like this is that you get to show him/her that you're not out to get him/her.

A lot of sincerity, patience, and trust is going to be needed in this phase. But as long as you both want to fix the relationship, it can happen. And as long as there seems to be a reasonable way of fixing things, you shouldn't give up on the relationship.

Chapter 4: Taking Time Apart

Let's say that both of you want to try and fix the relationship but it seems that, for one reason or another, you can't seem to even get to the negotiating table on equal terms. This is probably because there's already some degree of distrust between the two of you where, unlike the previous situation, you can't be objective with each other anymore. This development in the conflict could be the result of a number of things:

- The toxicity of the relationship is one where alleged lies, manipulations, and infidelity were the cause, such that it's hard to trust that either one of you will make fair statements;

- There could be something really bad that one or both of you have experienced (either from each other or other people) that makes it difficult to engage each other without letting your emotions take over; or

- You both have problems clearly articulating your concerns. This can happen, especially when you face the problem in the midst of other stressful situations (i.e. business is bad, your family is in a bad situation, personal life crisis). When you're juggling these things together, sometimes it's hard to organize your thoughts.

This is where the cooling off period comes in handy. Sometimes it's important for both of you to individually take a step back and go back to basics. Perhaps there's just too much on your plate right now that if you add the relationship problem to it, things will only get worse. In that case, you don't want your relationship to be caught in the middle of the crossfire.

Lots of people are afraid of taking time off, but there are a lot of good reasons why it can be healthy:

- You can focus on resolving other issues, especially when you know which ones are causing all the stress that you are transferring to your partner. This could allow you to go back to the negotiating table with more reasonable expectations and fairer judgment.

- You can think about the positive aspects of yourself, your partner, and the relationship. You'd be surprised at how we are inclined to harbor negative feelings when we are too close to the object of our negativity. The time off will let both of you see what you have taken for granted, and what you're missing when apart.

- You can safely think about whether it's time to let go. Sometimes you can't think about severing the relationship when the person you are trying to let go of is right in front of you. That's because you're either scared of the consequences or you don't want to feel like you're abandoning the person.

- The corollary of this is that the time apart could itself help you change your mind about leaving the relationship or, at least, how you feel about the last thing you fought about.

Remember that the cooling off period is the period between the time when you both try to fix the relationship and when you finally decide to let go. At this point, you're getting a lot of "me time" but at the same time, you're still putting your partner in the equation—without the pressure or toxicity. At this point, it's very important to be completely honest with yourself. If you can come up with a bright idea on how to fix the relationship once the period is over, that's good. But if you realize that it's the end of the

27

line and you need to move to the next chapter of your life, then at least you can tell yourself that you really thought about it and didn't act on impulse.

Chapter 5: Letting Go as a Last Resort

This is it. You've tried fixing the relationship, but nothing helped. You've taken some time off, and you realize that you stand to lose more than gain in keeping the relationship. It's come to this. It's got to end.

At this stage, the opinion of your partner isn't going to matter as much as your own. You need to end this, one way or another. But if you were able to pull off talking it out and doing the cooling off period, you can get out of this whole thing unscathed. If you're lucky, your partner could have thought of breaking it off as well, for his/her own reasons.

And while letting go isn't easy, you can do a couple of things to make it less difficult:

- First, you'll want to meet with the other party in a neutral place. It's preferable to go somewhere semi-public, especially when the reason for cutting ties is abuse. You might be safer in a public place.

- Second, go to the venue prepared with what you have to say. Rehearse it if you must. When explaining why the relationship should end, you can try going back to what you've talked about in the past. **Note:** Although whether or not your partner will agree with you may not matter to you anymore, you need to make an effort to make him/her understand where you are coming from.

- Once you've stated your case, you will want to give the other party a chance to react to the situation. Don't just say you want to end it and walk away. After all, you could have missed something that could have changed your decision. This is the part where you take it slow.

- Assuming that the whole thing hasn't gotten violent, you need to start laying down some rules with your partner. Both of you will have wishes or requests with each other, such as what you should say or not say to common friends or family, or what the time frame will be for one of you to move out from your shared space.

At this point, all you can really do is walk away. If you've reached this point without anything escalating unreasonably, pat yourself on the back because you were able to get out of the relationship without too much damage.

But it's not over yet, because escaping the relationship is only half the battle. You have to sustain the separation by changing routines and lifestyles that involve the former relationship. This means deleting contacts and maybe disconnecting from social networks, depending on what you agreed upon.

Should the other party be unaccepting of the situation and continue to try to reach you, you might want to try going away for a while so that you are given the time you need to be alone to recover.

Note: If the relationship was abusive, don't hesitate to ask for help from law enforcement authorities in securing your safety.

You can also attend support groups who can help you move on faster. Some people are ashamed of resorting to this, but you need to realize that there's nothing to be ashamed of. In fact, your willingness to admit the end of a relationship and ask for help to recover is a sign of maturity and strength.

Undoubtedly, you've done the right thing. But now, you need to focus on pulling yourself together and getting on with your life. It's going to take a while, but there's no pain in this world that time cannot heal.

Conclusion

While it's true that you may have contributed to the loss of the relationship, you need to remember that some relationships simply come and go. That's how life works. And as long as you remember that you yourself are not perfect, coming to terms with losing people you thought were important in your life will not be impossible.

Don't ever forget to forgive yourself. Not everything is in your control, and that includes toxic relationships. In fact, it would have probably been more unforgivable if you stayed in a relationship that hurt more than helped you grow as a person.

Finally, share your newfound knowledge with other people. Just like you, people you may know will experience toxic relationships in their lives as well. When the opportunity arises, make it a point to objectively help your loved ones either overcome the hurdles that threaten to doom their relationships, or help them get out of their own failing relationships as well.

Getting out of a toxic relationship is never easy. But nothing in life that makes you a better person ever is.

By knowing which relationships to hold on to and which ones to let go of, you get to focus on the people who really matter, making life that much more precious.

Finally, I'd like to thank you for purchasing this book! If you found it helpful, I'd greatly appreciate it if you'd take a moment to leave a review on Amazon. Thank you!

Made in the USA
Lexington, KY
22 December 2016